FASHION HACKS

TIPS TO UP YOUR WARDROBE

BY LISA M. BOLT SIMONS

CAPSTONE PRESS
a capstone imprint

Published by Spark, an imprint of Capstone
1710 Roe Crest Drive, North Mankato, Minnesota 56003
capstonepub.com

Library of Congress Cataloging-in-Publication Data
Names: Simons, Lisa M. B., 1969- author.
Title: Fashion hacks : tips to up your wardrobe / by Lisa M. Bolt Simons.
Description: North Mankato, Minnesota : Spark, an imprint of Capstone, [2023] | Series: Life hacking! | Includes bibliographical references and index. | Audience: Ages 9-11. | Audience: Grades 4-6. | Summary: "Are you tired of your basic T-shirt? Looking to upgrade your footwear? There's no need to spend big bucks when you can fashion hack it! Flip through these pages to learn how to take your everyday look and make it pop! Easy-to-read, high-interest hacks will engage even the most reluctant reader"— Provided by publisher.
Identifiers: LCCN 2022004703 (print) | LCCN 2022004704 (ebook) | ISBN 9781666354171 (hardcover) | ISBN 9781666354188 (pdf) | ISBN 9781666354218 (kindle edition)
Subjects: LCSH: Clothing and dress—Remaking—Juvenile literature. | Fashion—Juvenile literature.
Classification: LCC TT550 .S56 2023 (print) | LCC TT550 (ebook) | DDC 646/.3—dc23/eng/20220223
LC record available at https://lccn.loc.gov/2022004703
LC ebook record available at https://lccn.loc.gov/2022004704

Editorial Credits
Editor: Mandy Robbins; Designer: Dina Her; Media Researcher: Jo Miller;
Production Specialist: Tori Abraham

Image Credits
Getty Images: Allison Cherry, 26, Karisssa, 8, Vladimir Vladimirov, 17; Shutterstock: adutt, 18, AinurKas111, 12 (tape), baldezh, 16 (spoon), Balora, 28 (hand cleaning), BAZA Production, Cover (girl, boy), BearFotos, 5, Boris Medvedev, 15 (right), Chiyacat, 13, Crystal01, 15 (left), deep purple design, 9 (both), 10, Francesco Milanese, 14 (split ring), Garage133, 23 (boots), hem28, 16 (ribbon), imtmphoto, 29, Karbo_Kreto, 4 (all), 6 (shirt), Kartinkin77, 21, Khvost, 7 (shirt), laschi, 20 (shoes), lineartestpilot, 20 (dryer), Magdalena Wielobob, 11, Mega Pixel, 23 (marker), 24, mocker_labs, 19 (slippers), Natcha Yamkasamkul, 6 (spray bottle), nikiteev_konstantin, 28 (cap), nui7711, 14 (jeans), Pixel88, 7 (tie dye), RadikSunShine, 25 patches), Sintcova Svetlana, 20 (candle), SOORACHET KHEAWHOM, 22, suesse, 19 (hook and loop fastener), TheBlackRhino, 16 (cup), Twinsterphoto, 25 (girl, backpack), vectorisland, 10 (scissors), 12 (scissors), 27 (scissors), yellow design, 27 (shirt), Zholobov Vadim, 12 (jeans)

Design Elements
Shutterstock: ARTvektor, Apostrophe, Djent, frescomovie, impress, laschi, Karbo_Kreto, mhatzapa, ta_samaya,

All internet sites appearing in back matter were available and accurate when this book was sent to press.

Printed and bound in the USA. PO4882

TABLE OF CONTENTS

Words in **bold** are in the glossary.

SHORTCUTS TO STYLE

Who has time for fashion? You do! With a hack, or shortcut, your clothes can highlight your best features. Make a basic T-shirt pop. Get the best fit fast. **Upcycle** old shoes and accessories for brand new looks.

TRICKS TO TOPS

Hack your top with a **bleach** design. This household cleaner will make bright designs on dark tees. Just make a paper **stencil**. Place it on top of a tee and spray with bleach. Watch your design come to life! For an easier project, draw designs with a bleach pen.

Want a pro tip? Put a piece a cardboard or plastic inside your tee. This keeps your design on one side.

SAFETY NOTE

Ask an adult for help using bleach. It is a strong chemical.

Want a better-fitting top? Use knots! You can tie them in the front, side, or back.

Shirt too long? Tie a knot on each side. Too wide? A front knot can fix that. If you want to hide your knot, tie it in the back.

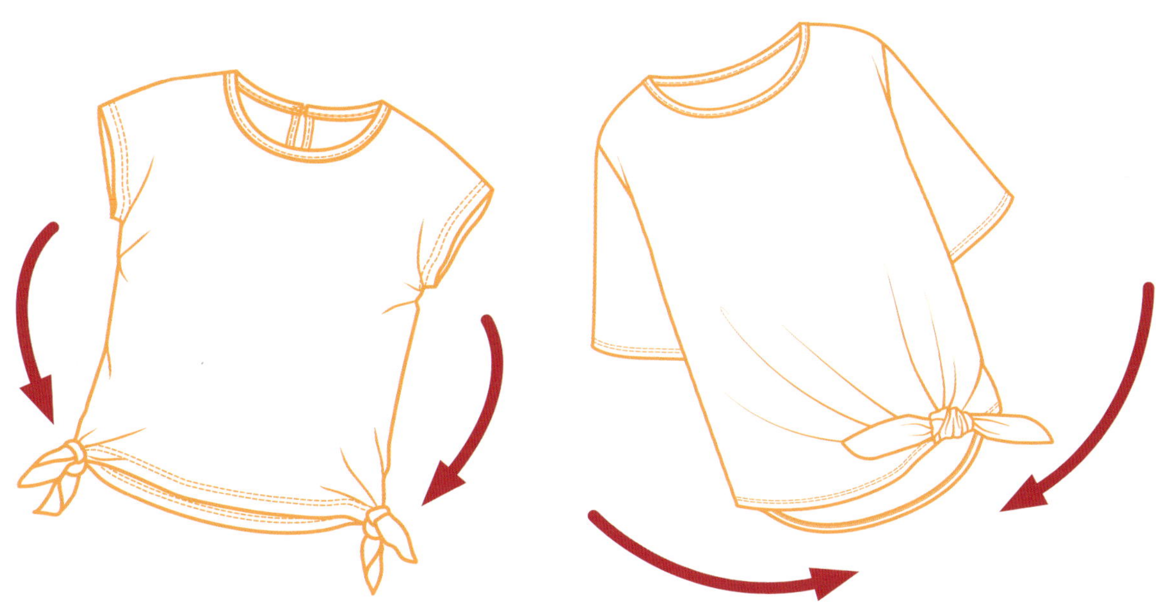

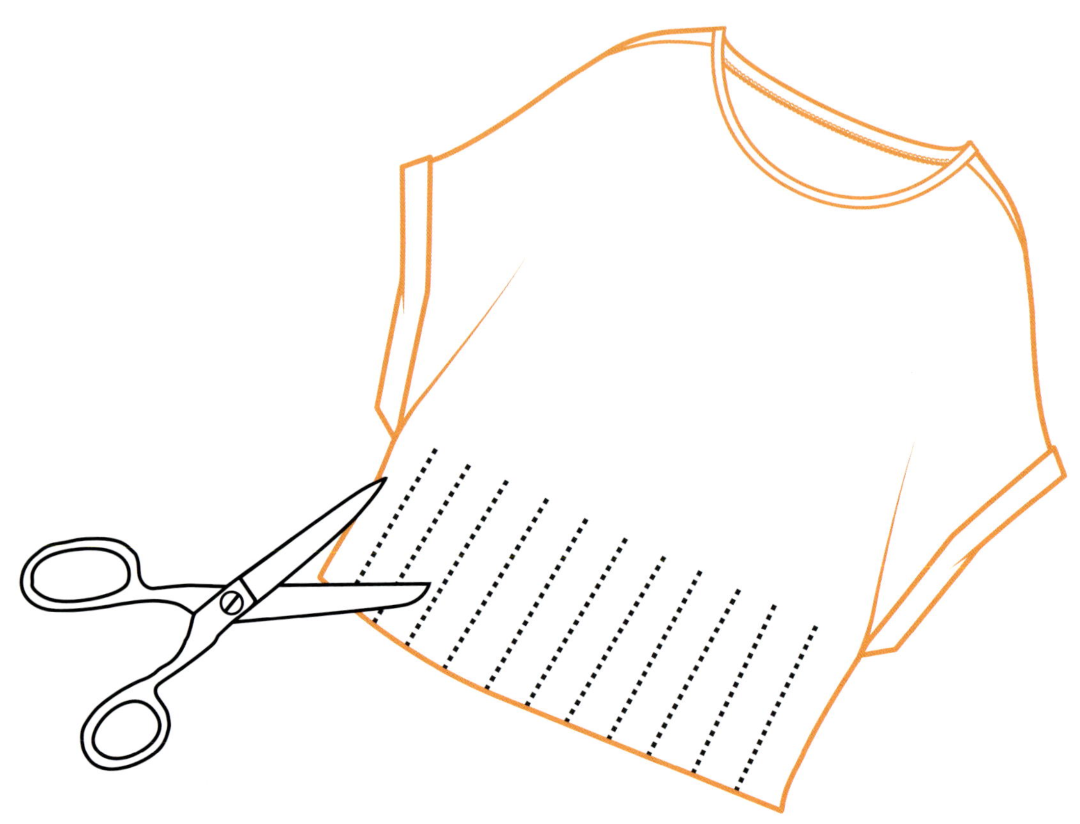

Add fringe for an edgy look. Lay the shirt flat on a table. Line up the bottom edges. Cut strips of fringe any length you want. Tie the fringe pieces together. Or tie a knot at the top of each piece too. You can even add fringe to shirt sleeves.

BETTER BOTTOMS

Shortcut for shorts? Cut off an old pair of pants! Fold jeans up for a neater look. For other fabric, add a **hem**. Turn the shorts inside out. Stick hem tape on the bottom edges. Fold the hem and iron.

FACT

Astronauts hack their dirty underwear. They launch it into space to burn!

Does your zipper keep sliding down? Use a key ring! Slide it on the zipper and hook it over the button.

Are your leggings too long? Pull up the **material** until the cuff is where you want it. Then fold the extra material down over the cuff. Fold the cuffs up for a different look.

STYLIN' SHOES

Want eye-catching shoelaces? Try this hack.

Make your shoelaces glow in the dark! Mix **tonic water**, a capful of **peroxide**, and a spoonful of baking soda. Soak white shoelaces for five minutes. Dry. Lace your shoes and turn off the lights.

STYLE TIP!

You can use ribbon as shoelaces too. Wrap the ends with tape to get the ribbon through the shoelace holes.

Would you like flip-flop options? Get a pair of plain flip-flops. Attach fabric **swatches** to peel-and-stick Velcro. Use fabric, leather, or **suede** swatches. Stick them on the flip-flops. Swap them out for different styles.

Want to waterproof your canvas kicks? Get a plain white candle. Rub it over every inch of your shoe. Use a hair dryer to melt the wax. Once the wax dries, no water will soak through your shoes.

Make old shoes look new. Load up a toothbrush with whitening toothpaste. Use it to scrub white sneakers clean. Soak the laces in water and toothpaste.

Are scuffed black shoes getting you down? Use black permanent marker to fill in the scuffs. Bam! Your shoes look new.

AWESOME ACCESSORIES

Ditch your boring backpack. Use permanent markers to draw designs on a plain backpack. You can also use fabric paint.

Trying to cover up a stain or tear? Stitch or iron on a patch to create a fresh new look.

Upcycle old T-shirts to make stylish totes! Turn a T-shirt inside-out. Cut off the sleeves and neck. Then cut two inches off the bottom. Gather the material. Tie it with the strip you cut off the bottom. Turn it right-side-out, and it's ready to go.

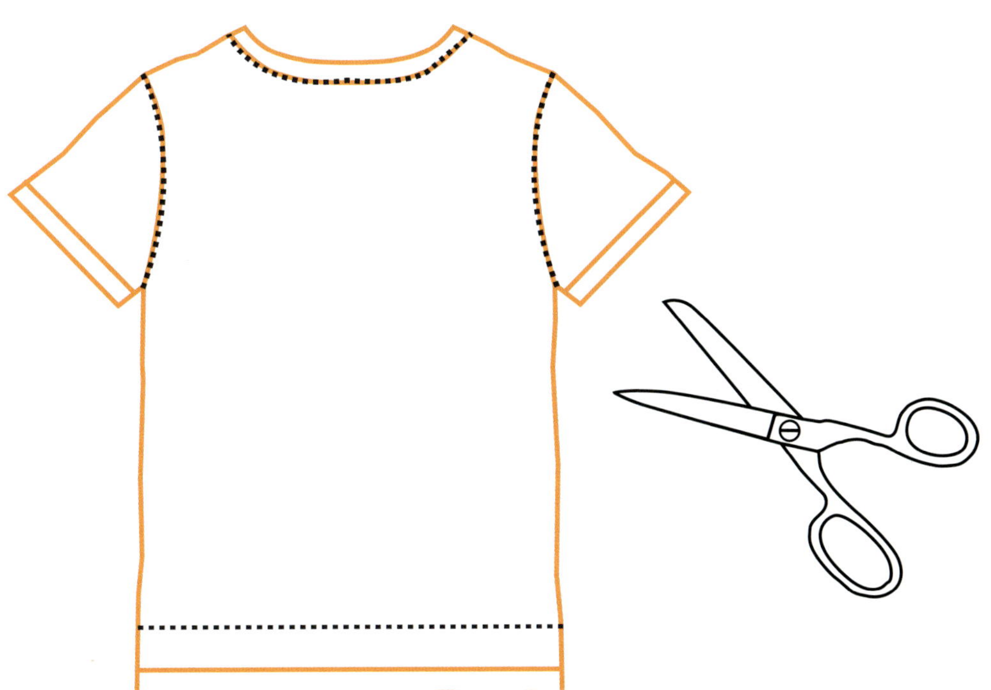

Get stains and stink out of ball caps. Soak your cap in lemon juice and warm water. Then scrub it with dish soap and air dry. Or brush on a paste of baking soda and water. Add a few drops of vinegar and rinse. Wash with dish washing soap and air dry. Now you're ready to step out in style!

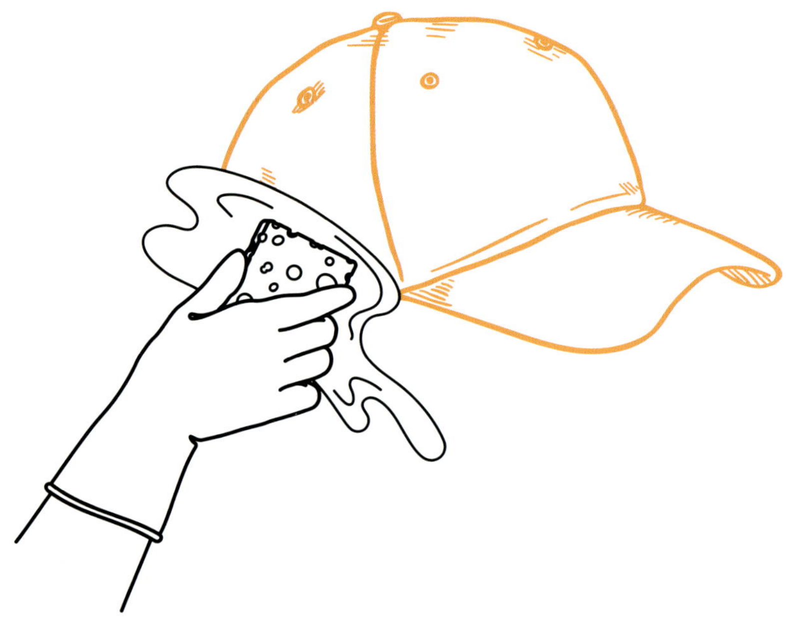

GLOSSARY

bleach (BLEECH)—a chemical used to remove color

hem (HEM)—the edge or border of cloth, usually at the bottom

material (muh-TEER-ee-uhl)—fabric or cloth that clothing is made from

peroxide (pur-OKS-ide)—a strong chemical that can clean and bleach items

stencil (STEN-suhl)—a piece of material that has a pattern or design cut out of it

suede (SWAYD)—soft leather with a velvetlike surface

swatch (SWOCH)—a sample of cloth or material

tonic water (TAH-nik WAH-tur)—a kind of carbonated water

upcycle (UHP-sye-kuhl)—to make something from an already used item

READ MORE

Delisle, Raina. *Fashion Forward: Striving for Sustainable Style*. Custer, WA: Orca Book Publishers, 2022.

Fontichiaro, Kristin. *Hacking Fashion: Denim*. Ann Arbor, MI: Cherry Lake Publishing Group, 2017.

Rissman, Rebecca. *Fashion Hacks: Your Fashion Failures Solved!* North Mankato, MN: Capstone, 2018.

INTERNET SITES

5 Fashion Hacks to Keep Kids Cool This Summer
khaleejtimes.com/city-times/5-fashion-hacks-to-keep-kids-cool-this-summer

15 Epic Hacks for Old Kids' Clothes
momtastic.com/health-wellness/kid-style/616775-hacks-for-old-clothes/#/slide/15

33 Clothing Hacks That Will Save You a Lot Of Money
lifehack.org/articles/money/33-clothing-hacks-that-will-save-you-lot-money.html

INDEX

ABOUT THE AUTHOR

Copyright Jillian Raye Photography

Lisa M. Bolt Simons has published more than 50 nonfiction children's books. She's twice received an Honorable Mention for the McKnight Artist Fellowship for Writers in Children's Literature. She's also received two Minnesota State Arts Board grants. Lisa is a proud mom to twins. Originally from Colorado, Lisa lives in southern Minnesota with her husband.